John Pritchard

Sermon Occasioned By The Death Of The Late Capt. Webb

John Pritchard

Sermon Occasioned By The Death Of The Late Capt. Webb

ISBN/EAN: 9783744651486

Printed in Europe, USA, Canada, Australia, Japan

Cover: Foto ©Thomas Meinert / pixelio.de

More available books at **www.hansebooks.com**

A SERMON,

OCCASIONED BY

The Death

OF THE LATE

CAPT. WEBB;

And Preached at

PORTLAND-CHAPEL, BRISTOL,

DECEMBER 24, 1796,

At the Time of his Interment.

BY JOHN PRITCHARD.

" And they that be wise shall shine as the brightnefs of the firmament, and they that turn many to righteoufnefs, as the stars for ever and ever." DAN. xii. 3.

" Servant of God, well done, well haft thou fought
The better fight———
                    For this was all thy care
To stand approv'd in sight of God, though worlds
Judg'd thee perverse." MILTON.

BRISTOL:

PRINTED AND SOLD BY R. EDWARDS, BROAD-STREET;
Sold alfo by B. Crofby, Stationers'-Court, London; Hazard, and Gould,
Bath; Wafhbourn, Glocefter; Bafkerfield, Worcefter; Grafton and
Reddle, Birmingham; Penny, Exeter; Harry, Truro; Hayden,
Plymouth; and by other Bookfellers in Town and Country.

1797.

[PRICE SIX-PENCE.]

SERMON.

ACTS xx. 24.

But none of these things move me, neither count I
my Life dear unto myself, so that I might finish
my Course with Joy, and the Ministry which I
have received of the Lord Jesus.

WE have now an occasion, by the death and departure to glory of our much-loved and highly-revered
Brother, to contemplate the character of a minister of
Christ Jesus; of an instrument who is employed to turn
men from the error of their ways into the paths of holi-
nefs, from the fervice of idols to worship the living and
true God, in order that they may partake of his life,
and live and reign with him to all eternity.

The greatnefs of this object, together with the energy
required for profecuting it, and the difficulty of accom-
plifhing it, can only be counterbalanced by the affurance
of deriving fufficient aid from above. The obftacles in
the apoftle's way were very great, verfe 23. *The Holy*
Ghoft witneffeth in every city, faying that bonds and
afflictions abide me. But what are his fentiments on
this trying feries of diftreffes? Such as become the Chriftian Hero :—*But none of thefe things move me, neither*

A 2   *count*

count I my life dear unto myself, so that I might finish my course with joy. Is this all ? no :—This selfish object had not powers adequate to carry him through the projected difficulties, and therefore he couples with it the consideration, without which he could not have *finished his course with joy;*—viz. that he might also finish the *Ministry which he had received of the Lord Jesus.* This was the darling object and grand desire of the Apostle, which exposed him to the most imminent dangers ; and notwithstanding he foresaw that he should fall by the command of *Nero,* and end his race in blood, yet he rejoices to think *that Christ should be magnified in his body, whether it be by life or by death.*

The text necessarily induces us to take a view, (which we will in a summary way,)

First, Of the great difficulties attendant on a Christian Ministry.

Secondly, Of the Minister's support under them. And

Thirdly, I shall consider their particular application to our late Brother, whose remains lie before you.

And *First.* As we cannot more accurately state the difficulties than St. Paul himself, we will do it from his own enumeration of them—2 *Cor.* xi. 23. and in *Eph.* vi. 12. *We war not only against flesh and blood, but against* those things and evil principles, which actuate them, *against principalities, against powers, against the rulers of the darkness of this world, against spiritual wickedness in high places.* All persons cannot do all things, it is

not

not every Preacher who has every one of thefe to encounter, though the great Apoftle had. As he had to contend againft *Principalities*, fo the Minifter whofe fphere of labour is moft narrow has to contend againft fome provincial, fome parochial, fome diftrict or family idol, which lifts up its head as proudly as any imperial Dagon, againft being brought into fubjection to the obedience of Chrift. The monopolizing farmer, the fyftematically overreaching tradefman or lawyer, in lower walks of life; in the higher ranks, the habitual gambler, the authorized oppreffor of the poor, and the proud defpifer of the meek and humble, the adulterer, the fornicator, the befotted drunkard; the Sadducees, Pharifees and Atheifts, with many others, have each erected an ufurped principality independant of God and Religion, and deftructive to Man; and thefe principalities every one that preaches Chrift, is bound to attack. And he muft not expect to find them without *Powers* to fupport them, though each may have little ftrength by himfelf; though the drunkard may not be able to frame a fyllogifm for his defence; though the gambler may hefitate to fay as the chriftian can and does, that he proceeds on a certainty, or though the monopolizer of the means of human fubfiftence may be loth in words to allow his being connected with the workers of iniquity, yet each will rufh in to the aid of the other. There is a general alliance offenfive and defenfive among thefe petty principalities which is moft rigidly adhered to; and no fooner is any one blocked up in his caftle and unable to fally out, but the others lead out their powers in his defence and fall upon the chriftian affailant in flank and rear.

Thefe

Thefe together are a confederate body, who fit as a
cloud brooding general *darkness in the world* of
which they are the *rulers,* and by their compact order
and zealous aid to every weak part, fhut out the light of
the gofpel, left it fhould fhine into their hearts. As the
aggregate is confiderable, it prefents a very extenfive field
of military operation, and requires a large force capable
of extending with effect in any direction, well fupplied,
ftrictly difciplined, and of undoubted courage, prudence,
abilities and perfeverance. The *high places* of the earth,
as *courts* and *camps*, or the high places of religion, as *Pon-
tificates* and their dependencies, are only fo many powers
that in all ages have oppofed the true Minifters of Chrift
and their place is the darknefs of this world. They will
not come to the light nor admit the light to them, left their
deeds fhould be reproved. It is hard to attack *principalities,* difficult to ftand our ground againft their *powers,*
almoft hopelefs to attack the ufurped authority of antichrift ; but it requires courage indeed to form and
conduct an attack upon thefe when they have not
merely arrived at their high places, their ftrong
ground; but are committing wickednefs there, and not natural wickednefs only, but *fpiritual wickednefs,* which
announces the Spirit of Truth and *every thing that is
called God* to be the immediate object of infult.

The Chriftian Minifter finds it difficult to advance the
divine life in the fouls of thofe whom Providence has
placed more immediately under his care ; to make religion fway and prevail; to frame and mould their minds
into conformity to the will of God, by enlightening the underftanding, rectifying the will, and fanctifying the affec-
tions. Nothing below this fhould be our aim ; neither
fhould

should we rest until this be accomplished. If any think this an easy work, let them try their skill on any person addicted to vice, and know for themselves if it be so. Persuade the drunkard to leave his cups, the covetous his hoards of gold, and the flaunting gallant to become serious. The bad examples, likewise, thatenveigle ourhearers greatly obstruct us :—We see them seldom ; but their companions often ; we bring them to some degree of sobriety for the time they are with us, but too soon it is worn off again by their wicked neighbours, who meet them every day, and by their bad example obliterate every good impression which the gospel has made on them. The foolish desires and hurtful tempers which they endeavour to hide from us, make the work of pious Ministers difficult. The Physician that attends to their health has all the advantage of us. When he enquires into the nature of their disorders, they are careful to give him all the information they can : but alas! when the Physician of their souls, (under God) enquires after their particular vices, they are as careful to hide them : thus it becomes difficult to detect these and administer to them. The public exercise of the ministry hath its difficulty. This is a work many are fond of, and none more so than those least qualified for it. It is no small matter to accommodate ourselves to the capacity of our hearers ; so as not to disgust any by insipid flatness in our addresses, and to awaken and rouse drowsy souls, without terrifying tender consciences ; to bear home particular sins, without the appearances of personal reflection : in a word, to prove ourselves workmen that need not be ashamed. The discipline of Christian Societies is a farther exercise, and is a kind of edge tool; and they need be wise who handle it. It is hard to manage the censures of the church with such prudence, that may
neither

neither encourage the flagitious finners by remiffnefs, nor
tempt to anger others by needlefs feverity ; nor give advantage to captious and troublefome men, for want of le-
gal formality. But the moft trying, is that of addreffing
ourfelves to each perfon. This, to fome bafhful and
humble minds is next to martyrdom. All which, confi-
dered in the aggregate, calls aloud for all poffible circum-
fpection, activity, and refolution, of which the Apoftle
was an exemplary inftance. This leads us,

Secondly, To confider the fupport of Minifters under
their difficulties.

That the Apoftle had confiderable fupport is plain,
when he faid, *None of thefe things move me!* No! not
though you ftand alone, and are confeffedly fent as a fheep
among wolves ? then you cannot be acting on any earthly
fupport, for all earthly powers are againft you. You are
fingly in arms againft a whole deluded and deluding world.
You are mad, or elfe you are divinely fupported from
above! Such is the cafe with every Minifter of Chrift.
*The weapons of our warfare are not carnal, but mighty
through God to the pulling down of ftrong holds, cafting
down imaginations, and every high thing that exalteth itfelf
againft the knowledge of God, and bringing into captivity
every thought to the obedience of Chrift:* Such were the
Apoftle's weapons! And fuch the GOD that inftructed
and fuftained him in the ufe of them! That he
was not deferted at his need, nor deluded with vain
promifes of fupport, we have his own evidence for, which
muft be received on every rule as difinterefted and com-
petent, efpecially at a moment *when he was ready to
be offered up, and the time of his departure was at hand.*
                                                 I have

I have fought a good fight : I have finished my course : I have kept the faith. Henceforth there is laid up for me a crown of righteousness, which the Lord, the righteous Judge shall give me at that day, and not to me only, but unto all them also that love his appearing.

This Scripture suggests to us two specific views of the support, which the Apostle received. The first of these we also find in the text, and it is that *Joy* or satisfaction and delight of the mind being at rest in Jesus, which the Apostle experienced, and which awaited him in its fulness of fruition in the successful issue of his battles, toils, and labours, which being conformed to those of his Lord, and having obtained like precious faith with the saints of old, in the blood and righteousness of Jesus Christ, gave him a title to Heaven, to enter his joy, and to sit down with him on his throne, even as he also had overcome and was set down with his Father on his throne. This is a powerful motive to exertion, and being a reward freely promised, may be claimed without presumption. For who is so fastidious to cavil with such a motive, when the Captain of our Salvation, for the joy that was set before him, endured the cross ?

But the second specific view that supported the Apostle, was more grand, definite, and extended. He looked to the perfection of his work and glory in the re-appearing of his Lord and Saviour Jesus Christ, who should himself give him a crown of glory, and not as a king, who has favourites, but as a J U D G E (Judge of his race); and who should *change his vile body, that it may be fashioned like unto his glorious body, according to the working*

B

whereby he is able even to subdue all things unto himself.

Till this event, the consummate joy and glory of the Apostle remain incomplete. Having a full and general commission, he could indeed assail and shake spiritual wickedness in high places; the Diana of Ephesus, the Areopagus of Athens, the Sanhedrim of Jerusalem, with the whole counsel of Priests and Elders, the Synagogue of the Libertines, and Cyreneans, and Alexandrians, together with them of Cilicia, and of Asia, so that they were not able to withstand the wisdom and spirit by which he spoke; yea and Rome, the Capital of the world, where idolatry sat on the throne of emperors, marched at the head of armies, and commanded all that was worldly, wise, or mighty. And all the terrible *Massacres* and executions done by it, neither did nor could prevail against a cause designed to teach suffering, to be carried on by suffering, and lastly to conquer all by suffering. In a word, religion founded on the cross, cannot be suppressed by the cross.

Here it is proper to remark, what is perhaps more extraordinary, *none of these things moved him*; but he still looked for his crown from the Lord, the righteous Judge. O! the sublimity of the christian! in whose view, both the splendid magnanimity, and the persecuting malice of imperial Rome, alike vanished into empty air!

Other Ministers, I have observed, have less general commissions from above. And yet there requires an illimitable commission before the Gentile world is subdued. The Apostle was enabled to shake all the ramparts, but
not

not allowed to take poffeffion. Even principalities and powers were not all made fubject to him. And it is evident in the prefent day, that fo numerous are the enemies, fo powerfully combined, and fo audacious, that they laugh at every thing facred and divine. Sometimes Chrift's Minifters are jeered and pointed at, as fo many fools and babblers. But why do not thefe profound rabbies, thefe oracles of reafon among the modern philofophers, baffle and repel thefe upftart babblers, and crufh their abfurd doctrine in the bud? It is eafier to contradict than confute. In fact, they are perpetually railed at as deceivers and impoftors, even while they are undeceiving the world from the delufions that fo univerfally bewitch it.

So rank is the foil of the world, that tares fpring up under the very hands of the reapers. It is time, O God, to put forth thine hand! It is high time for the Lord of the vineyard to come, and miferably deftroy the hufbandmen that deftroy the earth; to eradicate the fpiritual wickednefs in high places which has killed the Son, that the vineyard may be their own: and being POWERS, will yield to nothing but omnipotent POWER. Therefore the Son of Man fhall come with power, and with great glory, as his holy Prophets have predicted, his Apoftles have expected, and himfelf has promifed. God will come in his chariot as a whirlwind, to render his anger with fury, and his rebuke with flames of fire; to put down all his enemies; when the kingdoms of this world will become the kingdoms of our God and of his Chrift; who will reign among his ancients glorioufly for ever and ever.

Let us now, *Thirdly*, confider how far our deceafed friend, in his fphere, followed the Apoftle as he followed Chrift.   B 2   And

And as I have slightly touched upon one of the best of characters, I shall crave your attention and patience, while I propose to your farther imitation, one of the greatest examples of this kind in our day; I mean, that of our late friend, *Captain Webb*, who, being dead, yet lives, and ever will live in the memory of many here, and thousands besides. I do not intend to treat of him as is common in funeral *orations*. The history of his early part of life, may one day be drawn up by an abler hand. My work, at present, is to set him forth as a pattern of piety and true religion to MINISTERS and PEOPLE.

Capt. WEBB was in his younger days a very useful servant of the crown; in which situation he received a wound in his arm, and lost his right eye in the same campaign that *General Wolfe* lost his life. He was always a man of moral character, and much respected in the army as an officer and a friend. From the earliest dawn of reason upon his mind, he had frequent convictions from *that light which enlighteneth every man that cometh into the world*; his conscience accusing or excusing, according to his general conduct.

In the year 1764, being about forty years of age, it pleased that God who knoweth the heart of man, which in its natural state is deceitful above all things and desperately wicked, to convince him by the power of his Spirit *alone*, of this important truth, deeply impressing his mind with his awful situation as a fallen creature. Not having any *spiritual* friend at this time to advise with, it pleased God, who had begun this blessed work, to lead him in a very remarkable way to the knowledge of salvation by the remission of sins. He was frequently very much
distressed,

diftreffed, almoft to defpair ; fuffering grievoufly from
the temptations of Satan, who often fuggefted to his
mind, that there was no mercy for him, and tempted
him to put an end to his exiftence. While under this
temptation, in extreme agony of foul, he befought the
Lord to feal his doom, or direct him to fome comfortable
paffage of fcripture ;* when, with a trembling hand, he
opened the Bible, and caft his eye upon Ifaiah liv. 7, 8.
*For a fmall moment have I forfaken thee, but with great
mercies will I gather thee : In a little wrath I hid my face
from thee for a moment, but with everlafting kindnefs will
I have mercy on thee, faith the Lord thy Redeemer.* He
took great comfort from thefe words, and was fingularly
directed in a dream to a *Moravian Minifter*, (a Mr. *Cary*)
whom he met with on his way from London to Briftol,
and whofe perfon he knew as foon as he faw him, in con-
fequence of his dream; wherein alfo it had been fuggefted
to him, that *that man would lead him to Chrift.* As foon as
they arrived in this city, he took an opportunity of open-
ing his mind to Mr. *Cary*, who told him, he muft lie at
the feet of the Lamb, and be wafhed in his blood : giving
him at the time an invitation, which he accepted, to hear
him preach the next day. This was on March 23, 1765.
While the Minifter was fpeaking on the fufferings of
Chrift, and his love to mankind, it pleafed the Lord to
fet before him the crofs, and the Saviour of the world
bearing his fins in his own body on it ; when, in a moment, his burden was removed, peace and joy through
believing

---

* We do not wifh to countenance the practice of converting the Bible
into a Fortune-telling Book ; though we believe the Lord may often go out
of his general way to meet the wifhes of the fimple enquirer after his will.
Capt. WEBB, at this time, knew nothing of God's general dealings with his
people, or with the plan of falvation.

believing filled his mind ; having, according to the language of the Homily of the Church of England, "a divine
perfuafion, or confidence, that all his fins were blotted
out, and he reconciled to God by the merits of Chrift ;"
And, according to the language of fcripture, Rom. v. 1.
*Being juftified by faith, he had peace with God through our
Lord Jefus Christ.* Soon after this, it pleafed the Lord
to ftrengthen him with repeated tokens of his favour ; giving him a ull affurance of hope, that he fhould one day
be with him in glory, which affurance he enjoyed to the
day of his death, being more than thirty years.

He became acquainted with the Methodifts through the
late Rev. Mr. *Roquet* a few days after his converfion,
who introduced him to the acquaintance of feveral pious
people, among whom he found that fpirit and experience
which anfwered to his own, and which together with a divine
impreffion on his mind, whereof he often fpoke, determi-
ned him to live and die with thofe people.

The firft time of his bearing a teftimony of the truth
was in Bath ; when the preacher not coming as was expected, he was defired to fpeak to the people, which he
did, and gave an account of his own experience. This
was all he knew about preaching at that time, and the
people were much bleffed.

Soon after this he had occafion to go to *America* in his
military capacity, where he was appointed *Barrack-Mafter*
of Albany. As foon as he arrived there he made a point of
holding family prayer in his houfe, at which his neighbours
frequently attended; after a little while he ventured to give
them a word of exhortation, and from the good effects that
appeared

appeared in their converſion, he was encouraged to go farther ſtill, even into the highways and hedges.

This ſtar aroſe (for a ſtar he was of no ſmall magnitude,
if that ſaying be true, that "he is the greateſt preacher who
converts the moſt ſinners") at a time when pleaſure was
extending her alluring voice to enſnare; when infidelity
had almoſt overſpread the land, and religion was hardly
to be found. Unſupported by human aid; oppoſed by
prejudice, and error widely prevalent; by intereſt and
authority, wit and learning, in league to baffle his humble
labours, he ſtill ſucceeded.

This man (*of whom the world is not worthy*) from the
love he bore to the ſouls of men, iſſued forth like light-
ning from one end of the land to the other, to bind up the
broken hearted, and proclaim liberty to the captives. In
one place we ſee him breaking forth like a mighty tempeſt,
and thundering from mount Sinai upon the impenitent :
In another place we behold him, like a benificent cloud,
pouring the ſpirit of grace and conſolation in copious
ſtreams upon the mourners in Zion.

> " Rich bleeding love his glowing tongue inſpires,
> Fills his rapt boſom with ſeraphic fires!
> His heart elates! his nobleſt powers employs!
> Augments his fervours, and improves his joys!"

He came not out among us, like the philoſophical Divines
of the day, to teach us to number the ſtars, to know
their rounds, and to diſcover the ſecrets of nature; but to
convince his fellow ſinners of ſin, and of righteouſneſs,
and of judgment; to teach us that the world paſſeth away
and

and the fashion thereof; and that there is nothing more dangerous than forming an undue alliance with its cus-toms and fading pleasures. He came not among us to instruct us in state affairs, and rules of civil policy, which is frequently nothing but the art of deceiving ; but to difcipline us for heaven. Though a foldier by profeffion, he came not to infpire us with the love of conqueft and triumph, which animated the Alexanders and Cæfars of former times, and the heroes of the prefent age; but to conquer felf, and to inflame our minds with the love of Jefus and eternal happinefs.

The doctrines he taught, and for which he met the fier-ceft oppofition, were the fame that awakened the fcorn and rage of the world ever fince the beginning; and which many, who call themfelves chriftians, oppofe with all their zeal : fuch as, The Divinity of Chrift, and the Holy Spirit ; proving from the fcriptures and other re-cords, that they were one with the Father, whofe glory is equal, whofe majefty is co-eternal, and that the Church has always believed and maintained it. The *Holy Spirit* is not from himfelf as the *Father* is, for that being fuppo-fed, there would be more principles than one, confe-quently, more Gods than one, which is contrary to the whole tenor of the fcriptures. The *Father* muft be the firft principle of all effence, the *Son* in the *Father*, and the *Holy Spirit* deriving his effence from both, and repro-ducing them in the world, and in the heart of man.

The doctrine of Free and Univerfal Grace. He believed and taught us that the grace of God was free for every man. *That Jefus Chrift tafted death for every man*, and that in virtue of it, *a meafure of grace was given to every man*

to profit withal, and confequently that man is free to
choofe or refufe. For if a man cannot do that which is
lawful and right, he cannot do that which is unlawful and
wrong: for what he feems to do is done in him and for
him, either by irrefiftible depravity, or irrefiftible grace:
a doctrine in oppofition to fenfe and reafon, and conftant
experience, which convinceth us that we have a power
of acting and choofing. It can be no objection to this
truth that according to the fcripture we cannot pleafe God
without his affiftance; for this is fo far from being an
objection, that it is a proof of our freedom to accept of
fuch affiftance and to concur with it. For as a Divine of
the eftablifhed church faid, "*It muft be a barbarifm of language, to talk of affiftance to a creature that hath no activity or power of its own; it is like a man talking of affift-
ing a mere machine or a burthen that he takes up by
main force.*"

The doctrine of the Sinner's Juftification by Faith in
Chrift, without any refpect to works, but fuch as proceed
from that faith, and manifeft it. This is the one only
condition of our juftification the gofpel recommends, and
from which we cannot be excufed. *Thy faith hath faved
thee: faith hath made thee whole*; and again, *O woman,
great is thy faith.* Yet be it remembered, that fhe had firft
proved her faith by an *act* or *work* fpringing from it. In
prayer the fame condition is required ;—*whatfoever ye
fhall afk in prayer believing, ye fhall receive*; again,
*what things ye defire when ye pray, believe that ye
receive them, and ye fhall have them.* God requires
faith becaufe he hath given us abundant reafon to credit
his word. The light of nature (fo called) difcovers that
God is good: The gofpel reprefents him good and mer-

ciful

ciful beyond all expreſſion: moſt juſtly then he may re-
quire of us faith in his promiſes. Faith in the righteouſneſs of Jeſus Chriſt, is enjoined by the ſcriptures for our
juſtification; becauſe it is productive of the beſt effects,
and is the forerunner and guardian of all graces. It ſuf-
fers us not to be deceived by wordly hopes and fears, nor
by worldly notions of right and wrong. It influences our
conduct to ſeek God, when we believe that God is; and
it is ſaying in our hearts and lives, that we acknowledge
him to be all-knowing, wiſe, and good. *John* iii. 33.
*He that believeth his teſtimony hath ſet to his ſeal that God
is true.* In a word, there is no other way of ſalvation.
God is inviſible. No man hath ſeen him, nor can fee him.
To faith only is it given to behold the throne "dark with
exceſſive brightneſs," and to diſcover the glorious perfec-
tions that fill it! The principal reward is alſo like himſelf,
inviſible to the merely natural man : it lives in a diſtant
region which no eye hath ſeen, no foot hath trodden ;
and before we take poſſeſſion, we muſt leave *all* that the
worldly-minded man counts his all, and beyond which he
hath no views. To believe in Jeſus Chriſt thus con-
cealed ;—to confide in him as being good, merciful, and
faithful, under all the inconveniences of life ; and to truſt
to a diſtant period for our reward, and to believe it ſo as
to influence our conduct, is ſomething more than human.

The New Birth, or Regeneration of Heart, and entire
Sanctification of our Nature, was another of the truths of
of the goſpel which he maintained ; a doctrine which is
counted nonſenſe by ſome, and impoſſible to be attained,
by others. Modern divinity has for the moſt part found
a ſmoother path to tread in, than that our worthy friend
taught, and by which he himſelf was brought to the
                                                    knowledge

knowledge of Jesus Christ. This is the man, (in con-
nection with many other Ministers) that revived in our
day the doctrine of Regeneration and Sanctification, when
the poor doubtful enquirers after these truths were only
entertained with ingenious essays on the beauty of virtue,
the efficacy of benevolence, the dignity of the human
mind, and other favourite topics; sanctification, or the
kingly office of Christ to his church, he often observed
with pain, was too much neglected by many that stile
themselves the Ministers of Christ, who in order to ex-
tol his priestly office, degrade the princely dominion of
his spirit in the heart. There cannot be a more dangerous or fatal delusion than to imagine, that any thing in
Christ can avail for us, so as to bring us to heaven, unless
we ourselves are actually created anew in Christ Jesus.
The opinion of Christian perfection being unattainable in
this life, has been begot and cherished by wild schemes of
it. But he (from all that I could learn) never recommended to the church a fantastic or enthusiastic perfection;
nor any heights of religion but what many actually feel
and practice, by living as he did, unspotted by the pleasures, and unbroken by the troubles of this world; mo-
dest and serene, equal and heavenly minded in honour
and dishonour, in want and abundance; in liberty, and in
prison; in death, and in life.

The doctrine of Atonement was forcibly inculcated by
him. Christ's Incarnation was his entrance into his office as
Mediator; for before this there was no law given, but by
the divine nature in the second person: Now the second
person, as God, is not subject to, but coequal with God
the Father. It was at Christ's free choice whether he
would be incarnate, or not; for he that is under law is
not at liberty to choose. Christ was under no law till he

became

became incarnate; he then, and not before, was a middle perfon, confequently became fubjeft to his Father. Nor can we fay Chrift was Mediator, but as God and man. No doubt but his mediation availed for all that looked for his coming in the flefh ; and with all thofe who be- lieved in God according to the light of their difpen- fation, had its merciful virtue and effects, before he was born of his Mother *Mary*. Chrift freely bound himfelf to fulfil all righteoufnefs. He made him- felf amenable to the law of innocence as a creature, and was fubjeft to it in the ftricteft fenfe :—to the law of *Mofes* as a Jew, and therefore was obliged to be circum- cifed in obedience to that law. He bound himfelf to the law of Mediation as a Day's-man, to manage and tranfact all affairs between his Father and us finners, in order to effect an everlafting union and fellowfhip.

The great work of Chrift's Atonement I would ftate thus : Firft, that which refpects God the Father, and was directed more immediately to him, is what holds forth Chrift as our great High Prieft, and one to whom alone the character of Prieft belongs; for the true Church under the gofpel, cannot with propriety acknowledge any other perfon under this character, as he only hath engaged in the work of atonement ; and as fuch, all that he did with God and man, in the way of fatisfaction and interceffion, whereby he obtains grace and glory for finners, refpected God. Rom. iii. 25. Heb. ii. 17. The fecond part of his office is to fubdue rebellious man, and bring him again into fubjection and obedience to God. This Chrift doth as a Prophet by his Spirit, Word, and Minifters, inftruc- ting him in his duty to God and man.—Acts iii. 22.— Phil. ii. 5.—1 John ii. 6.—1 Pet. ii. 21.—Heb. xii. 2. The third and laft part of his office, is that of a King ;
making

making fuch laws as we are to be judged by at laft, and meanwhile governing us by them. *For God has fet him as King upon his holy hill of Zion.* This takes in the government of the Churches, with all the gifts and offices that pertain thereto. Chrift pleads with his Father for man, and through the virtue of his blood and righteouf-nefs, obtains mercy and falvation for him : and pleads with man by his word and fpirit, which charge us not to refufe him that fpeaketh.—Heb. xii. 25. Chrift alfo gives himfelf to God an offering for man.—Gal. i. 4.—Titus ii. 14.—Heb. viii. 3. And he obtains gifts of God for man.—Pfalm lxviii. 18.—Heb. iv. 16.—ix. 24. *Who of God is made unto us Wifdom, and Righteoufnefs, and Sanctification and Redemption,* (1 Cor. i. 30.) to the praife and glory of his grace ; God having fet him forth a propitiation, through faith in his blood.

Time, in fhort, fails me to expatiate upon the doctrines of the Fall, of Repentance, of Rewards and Punifhments, of a Final Judgment : all which he maintained for many years, with a chriflian-like fortitude and magnanimity. His abilities as a Minifter lay principally in awakening poor finners ; and he was mighty in faith and prayer.

The good qualities of this great man were not few. That he had his weakneffes, as moft affuredly he had, none were more ready to acknowledge than himfelf. His charity was unbounded. There was nothing in the wide circle of his acquaintance, of a charitable kind, that came under his notice, but his mite was always ready. He made it his bufinefs to feek out the poor and needy ; he improved all opportunities of ufefulnefs. He went to thofe who would

not

not, and to others who could not, come to him. The fatherlefs and widows lay near his heart. To thefe his actual charity was eminently diftinguifhed.

To convince you how much he deferves our love and regard, it is fufficient to explain, in a few words, the effects which his labours have produced fince he began his miniftry. He was, under God, the firft inftrument of planting Methodifm in America; and not fatisfying himfelf with the fuccefs of his own labours in Philadelphia, New York, and other places, he ftretched out his hands to the Britifh Conference, and prayed them, *" Come over and help us."* Minifters were accordingly fent from this country to America; and many were raifed up among themfelves, who are now mutually labourin gto bring down *Antichrift*, to reduce fin, and to erect the Saviour's kingdom upon its ruins. By him many, but a degree from the brute, enemics to church and ftate, have learned *to render unto Cæfar the things that are Cæfar's, and unto God the things that are God's.* Let us bring to mind what God has wrought for us, and for his Church among us, by this his fervant, whofe memory we now embalm with our tears. Has not the Angel of the Covenant, by him, brought many through the wildernefs into friendfhip with us, and caufed them to favour the things of the Spirit? He was the man that planted them in a well-ordered church, where they are quickened by God's grace through a lively and faithful miniftry, where the gifts of Chrift are watered by the powerful prayers of his faints, the preach-ing of his word, and the holy Sacraments ; where many run to and fro that knowledge may be increafed ; and where difcipline is for a wall and bulwark, and our hearts warmed by the communion of his faints. By his in-fluence Preaching-houfes were erected in New York, Philadelphia,

Philadelphia, and many other places in the wide continent
of America; and even this houfe (Portland-Chapel) he
was the firft and principal Agent in erecting.

O! worthy man of God! who is it that knew thee, and
did not love thee? Like fine gold, the more he was
tried, the farther he enriched; like the fea, the more he was
obferved, the more immenfe; like the firmament, the
more he was examined, the greater number of ftars appeared.
As gratitude abhors oblivion, and is a recording grace,
keeping catalogues of favours; fo it is a reward to itfelf,
and by thefe records it furnifheth the foul with matter for
the fweeteft employment and delights. O that I could
raife your hearts in thankfulnefs to the bountiful Donor for
fo burning and fo fhining a light, who has now quitted the
world to return to the bofom of God! A river that has
flowed back to its original fource :—a fun paft into another hemifphere. He is gone! The happy fpirit hath
taken its flight! He will not come to us, we may go to him.
O highly favoured man, why art thou taken away in this
unbelieving age? when God is looked upon as an idle
fpectator, when infidelity prevails among all ranks; when
the religion of Jefus is turned and twifted to coincide
with the Newtonian or any other philofophy, which may
be the favourite fyftem of the age, and when the fons of
men are queftioning the very exiftence of a God!

His Death, though fudden, was not unexpected by him:
he has frequently told many of his approaching diffolution.
And the laft funday but one he ftood near the communion
table, under which we are now going to reft his peaceful
remains, and fhewed the place, and fpoke of the manner
of his burial, obferving, " I fhould prefer a triumphant
death;

death; but I may be taken away fuddenly. However, I now I am happy in the Lord, and fhall be with him whenever he calls me hence, and that is fufficient."

A few weeks fince, he preached his laft fermon from this pulpit, in which he bore a teftimony of the truth of the bleffed gofpel. His public prayers in this place were heard by many of you laft Monday night, and you no doubt recollect his fervour of devotion. The next evening, about an hour before his departure, he prayed as ufual with his family, and recommended them to God. After ten o'clock he retired to bed in his ufual health, and foon after, taking leave of his beloved partner for the night, he obferved that his breath was bad; and in a few minutes, without a ftruggle or a groan, his happy fpirit refigned its habitation, and fled to the realms of eternal day!

Having gone through, in a brief manner, the leading features of this extraordinary character; his converfion and call to the miniftry; his firft coming among us; his breaking through the greateft difficulties; his work; his religious fentiments, and the leading doctrines which he taught; his diligence and felf-denial; his great faith, zeal, and love; his manner of preaching and ufefulnefs, &c. you will bear with me while I attempt the moft difficult tafk of all; that is, to perfuade both preachers and people to tread in his fteps.

Pardon me, my friends, if any of you are inclined to think I have faid too much of our greatly-efteemed Brother: impute it to my friendfhip and gratitude: for with him I have gone in and out among this people for many

years.

years. Whatever you may think, my thoughts are that we cannot well fay too much of him. "He was the wonder of many; a fingular chara&ter :—the admiration, and worthy the imitation of all ;" as was faid of the great and benevolent *Howard*. "Where is the man to be found fully qualified to fatisfy his numerous friends? the utmoft fkill of the firft mafters of eloquence is required; his grave fhould be ftrewed with the choiceft flowers of oratory, and his memory embalmed in the richeft and moft pathetic language." Happy man! his days are ended, and he is now above the reach of temptation :—He is fled to thofe happy regions of light and joy, where there is no death, nor forrow, nor crying, and where all tears are wiped from every eye. Should not the example of our deceafed friend animate us that preach to others? who in the courfe of his labours cultivated a good underftanding, and having grace in himfelf, obtained knowledge in divine things, and was thereby enabled to preach the word in a plain, obvious, and powerful manner. Let us follow him in the poffeffion of true religion, in faith and love, in refifting the fmiles of a bewitching, and the frowns of a cenforious world. Let us attend to our duty, that as the eyes of the people are upon us, we may feed the numerous flocks committed to our care; gather the lambs in our arms, and tenderly care for the young; comfort Zion, build up her wafte places, preferve the public peace, and keep the people in quietnefs and fubjeftion to the authority fet over us, that the Lord God may dwell among us, and delight to do us good.

All who knew the value of this great and good Man, muft needs partake of the common forrow which his death has occafioned : but what words can exprefs the pier-

D   cing

cing grief of one, who is left, by so tender a Husband, in the solitary state of widowhood! and with what compassion should we address our prayers to the *Father of mercies*, to support her under this heavy stroke. Yet let not her mind utterly refuse to be comforted, since it ought to be counted a favour of divine Providence, to have been related to so valuable a person; and since it has pleased God, for the mitigation of her trouble, to give her the satisfaction of witnessing his christian behaviour in sickness and health, prosperity and adversity, and of hearing so often the gracious words which proceeded from him; so as to give her just reason to believe, his righteous soul is now happy, waiting for the resurrection of his body, while she has good hope, through grace, in a little time, to finish her course with joy, and enter into that rest which he has already attained. *A Father of the fatherless and Judge of the widow is God, in his holy habitation.* When God sends his messenger death, and takes a dear beloved creature from our arms, the question is like that of our Lord to St. Peter, *Simon, lovest thou me?* Art thou willing to resign this thy companion and comfort at my call? Can you now practice what you have so often repeated in your closets, and in the sanctuary; " I am thine, Lord I am thine, all that I have is thine?" Or do you murmur and quarrel with his will and pleasure? What an astonishing proof of our sincerity is this, when with Abraham we can and do take our only Son Isaac at God's command and offer him up unto death! Your Husband has forsaken you in your sorrowful moments, and has left you and your dear children to mourn alone; he forsook you while drowned in tears, and overwhelmed in heart, and now can give you no more consolation. Our fathers where are they? our prophets

our

our teachers, our guides, they are gone! O then let this lead you from the world, now your earthly comforts and dependance are fo much diminifhed, let it lead you to a folid dependance upon God, your only and abiding friend, one that will ftick clofer than a brother.

Is the Society in grief becaufe of lofing their companion and friend?

Your aged Minifter is gone, to return no more till the fecond coming of our Lord. What can you do better than to live and die as he did? You will fee his tears, and hear his voice no more! This pulpit is never more to be honoured by him! His fteadinefs and indefatigablenefs will no more correct your indolence, nor his holy practice reprove your fins. No: he is gone to the world of fpirits, and his clay we fhall foon confign to the tomb! O! bring to mind his extraordinary humility, his hearty friendfhip towards his equals, his condefcenfion to his inferiors, his unbounded charity to the poor, his readinefs to forgive, his zeal for truth, his loyalty to his Prince, his attachment to the people he was united to, his univerfal love to all. Think what there is in this world that fhould make you fond of it. What is it but a land of fhades, of griefs and trouble; where one dear friend after another is ravifhed out of our arms! Happy Chriftian, who walked with God to the end of his days, and when he died left a perfumed name behind him, and thoufands to call him bleffed! Such is the example this renowned champion of the crofs has left us, and fuch we have yet living among us, befides thofe that have departed in the faith of Chrift; and not a few in this place, the brightnefs and favour of whofe name abide to this day among us as ornaments to re-

D 2   ligion.

ligion, and as a rich perfume to the gospel still preached and lived by many. And as there are many under divine impressions, who feel the drawings from above, who are enquiring after salvation, and who in the simplicity of their hearts mark the lives of those that profess to walk by the leadings of the Spirit; what manner of persons ought ye to be in all holy conversation and godliness? Let no part of your conduct be contradictory to the truth which he taught you, nor a stumbling-block in the way of the sincere enquirers.

Under your present circumstances, you should heartily pray for a continuance of the gospel, that you may receive spiritual improvement. You should walk worthy of your calling, labouring to be more useful, exhorting one another daily: considering the weakness of your nature, the purity and presence of God, the strictness and impartiality of a judgment to come, the importance of eternal happiness, and of its awful reverse, eternal misery! My hearty prayer to God is, that the removal of our dear Brother from this Church to the Church above, may be a lasting blessing to those who were his companions of late years; so as to fill up his place, having the cause and interest of our Redeemer near their heart; praying earnestly to God to bless the rising generation; to strengthen them in running the race that is set before them; to wait meekly and humbly before the Lord to whom they have resigned themselves; to be of good courage, hoping in God, who will be their strength and support in the evil day.

To you, my friends, that have attended his ministry of late years, but have not ventured to give him the right hand of church-fellowship, he still lifts up his voice and cries,

cries, *Is it nothing to you that the Saviour should die?* Confider ferioufly and frequently how foon the fafhion and grandeur of this world.paffeth away. He that looketh for, and hafteneth unto the coming of the day of God, will have no great relifh for the honors and pleafures of this life; nor will he be flothful or remifs, but in timely preparation for it, will lay out the ftrength and vigour of his mind; retrenching his needlefs expences, denying his pleafures, and will be content to be counted obfcure, mean, and contemptible. O! watch againft the ficklenefs and infirmity of your fallen nature, by which you have fo often mifcarried : confider well the bleft reward that awaits the righteous in another world. Be ftedfaft in that faith and hope which wait and long for the coming of our Lord. This will invite you often to take a view of Canaan, to fill your mind with the beauties and realities of eternity—the fecurity of its reft—the tranfport of its joys—the love of Jefus—the crowns of glory—the felicity of angels —the perfection of faints—the fruit of the tree of life, and the ftreams that water the paradife of God. Such like thoughts may be ufeful to wean you from the world, felf, and fin, to upbraid your lazinefs, and incline you to hear the words of Jefus founding in your ears, *What, can you not watch with me one hour?*—or thofe words to the Church of Laodicea, *To him that overcometh will I grant to fit with me in my throne, even as I alfo have over- come and am fet down with my Father in his throne.*

Finally, my brethren, the call is to all. Let us, there- fore, lay afide all our little differences of opinion, all ani- mofities, and let us unite in the common caufe of Chrift. Let us bear up, in the ftrength of our common Lord and Saviour, againft all adverfe fortune, fo that the darkeft
difpenfations

difpenfations may prove occafions for our graces to fhine
forth and illumine them. *Take the Prophets for an exam-*
ple of fuffering affliction and patience. The greateft faints
have had their trials in the way to heaven ; and all is con-
fiftent with the love of our heavenly Father, and the rela-
tion which we bear to him. God knows what he hath to
do, and the part we are to act, and what will be moft con-
ducive to our fafety in the way to heaven. *Affliction*
cometh not from the duft, neither doth trouble
fpring out of the ground. I formed the light,
and create evil. I the Lord do all thefe things.
Refign yourfelves to God, as having an unqueftionable dominion over you. *Behold he taketh away, who can hin-*
der? who can fay to him what doeft thou? If God's glory
is promoted by it, why fhould we be diffatisfied? It was
upon this ground David was dumb, and opened not his
mouth, becaufe the Lord did it. *It is far lefs than our*
iniquities deferve. Let us then bear the indignation of the
Lord, becaufe we have finned againft him. Confider, there
is no defence againft death, nor any way to efcape it.
There is no man that hath power over the fpirit to retain
the fpirit, neither hath he power in the day of death, and
there is no difcharge in that war. No wealth can bribe, nor
eloquence perfuade, nor cries, nor tears can move. *Riches*
profit not in the day of wrath. The ftrongeft gates, caftles
or guards are no fecurity. Not the eloquent orator, not the
fkilful phyfician, not the mighty warrior, can hold a foul in
life. Improve then your fhort and uncertain day ; for if
you are once turned off this ftage of action, you cannot
re-enter to add what was omitted, nor rectify what is amifs.
What grace you have to get, muft be got now. Pardon
of fin, peace of confcience, reconciliation with God, the
mortification of your corruptions, and renovation of your
nature;

nature; in short, whatever is neceſſary for your
eternal welfare, now is the time to obtain it, for, now
is the day of ſalvation! Let us look up therefore to the
heavenly Jeruſalem as real, great, and glorious, for our
ſuffering time will ſoon be over, our complaints removed,
our graces made perfect, and our warfare accompliſhed,
the body of death put off with our body of fleſh, all tears
wiped from every eye, and joys begin which ſhall endure
for ever. Amen, and Amen.

THIS Sermon *is published at the request of the late* CAPT. WEBB's *Friends :—Who being also desirous of perpetuating his Memory,* R. EDWARDS *intends publishing by Subscription,*

An ELEGANT PRINT,

(A STRIKING LIKENESS)

to be executed by an eminent Artist in London, from an original Painting.

Subscriptions are received by the Publisher, No. 61, *Broad-street, Bristol, and by the Persons who sell this Sermon.*

Subscribers of Half-a-Guinea *will be entitled to* Three *proof Impressions.*

☞ *Single Prints* Four Shillings *each.*

The Money to be paid on delivery of the Print.